MW00387123

REWRITING A NEW HISTORY
A Spiritual Path to Audacious Authenticity and Healing

HAVILAH MALONE
Illustrated by Zuri Scott

Proof Of What's Possible, Inc.

Los Angeles

Disclaimer:
The information in this book is not intended as medical advice. While the author may provide keen insight and understanding into health issues, they are not a medical doctor or health care professional. Nothing contained in this book is intended to diagnose or treat physical or psychological conditions, prescribe or perform medical treatment, or interfere or substitute for the treatment of medical or other professionals. You should consult with a healthcare professional prior to implementing any of the techniques or suggestions contained in this book. Its intention is solely informational and educational. You are solely responsible for deciding whether any of the information is suitable for your purposes and do so at your own risk. Although the publisher and the author have made every effort to ensure that the information in this book was correct at press time and while this publication is designed to provide accurate information in regard to the subject matter covered, the publisher and the author assume no responsibility for errors, inaccuracies, omissions, or any other inconsistencies herein and hereby disclaim any liability to any party for any loss, damage, or disruption caused by errors or omissions, whether such errors or omissions result from negligence, accident, or any other cause. You agree to release and discharge the publisher and the author from any and all claims or causes of action, known or unknown, arising out of the contents of this book. The use of this book implies your acceptance of this disclaimer.

Contents

Greetings Dear Reader,

      There are no coincidences in life. The fact that you are reading these words right now is by divine design. The strings that connect all things may be invisible to the naked eye, but they are very real and lead us along our path to the people, information, and resources that are specifically designed to assist us throughout our journey.

      So often, we fear the unknown and branching off into uncharted territory. Yet we were born to be explorers, to venture out in pursuit of our own path and create it along the way. We were born to Shine. Who better to realize your potential, reclaim your power, and reinvent yourself than YOU? We are creators well equipped for the task ahead.

      There are messages and signs all around us that we are in a time of significant change and transformation. If you are ready to peer beyond the veil in order to transcend your current circumstances and gain vital insight into the human condition, you have come to the right place. You are being called to action. And the Universe has lovingly crafted a message specifically tailored for you. May you receive it with an open heart, open mind, and open third-eye!

Havilah Malone

$$\dotfill$$

Introduction

$$\dotfill$$

MANY PATHS TO HEALING

Have you ever been given an assignment you thought was too big, too complicated, and way out of your league? With each step forward, you were second-guessing yourself more and more? Ultimately allowing fear to overcome you like the infamous bible prophet Jonah, you ran and hid, hoping you really wouldn't have to do what you were being called to do.

That was me! I thought I was brave, smart, accomplished, and I could do anything. What I didn't realize was the path to finding and fulfilling your purpose, healing, and becoming aligned with one's true self was going to be so fucking hard. We deserve to have all the big goals and dreams we set out for ourselves. But in order to get there, we must first stop settling and conforming to the life others want us to live that is not authentic to who we really are or want to be. That requires going on a healing journey that starts from within. When you dare to venture introspectively, you'll experience your passions and dreams come to life. In this book's epilogue, I offer you a simple formula called SHINE to empower you to do this and much more.

We all carry deep wounds, some from our own experiences and some that are ingrained in our cellular memory from ancestral trauma inflicted on generations before us. Most things that plague us, we aren't even consciously aware of. It is our job, like a detective, to become observers of ourselves in order to uncover these habitual behaviors, patterns of thought, and limiting beliefs. The key to stepping into our full potential is releasing the things that no longer serve us while embodying new ways of thinking and living that do.

Growing up in a middle-class African American household that was deeply rooted in religious tradition heavily influenced my beliefs and outlook on life. I learned the rules of engagement for our culture, and I knew the script very well. Instructions were given on what I was supposed to do with my life, what was considered *important, right, wrong, true, false,* as well as where the boundaries were for what I should and shouldn't want.

I was living in a box, and I didn't even know it. For the majority of my life, that box felt safe. That box was all I knew. When my questions started peering into topics outside of that box I was often given the encouragement to just believe, to just have faith, and to just keep following the path laid before me.

Deep within my soul, I was seeking alignment. Maybe you've felt this way before? As I got older, I began to feel restless. I felt like there was more. There were things that I didn't know and didn't understand. I wanted to explore other systems of belief, practices, cultures, and ways of thinking that could provide answers to my questions. What if I just tip-toed beyond the boundaries of this particular box I was living in? Would I be able to find myself?

We all have an internal guidance system – that voice that nudges you in one direction or another, that vision, feeling, or knowing that you have deep inside that tells you this is a good decision or a bad decision. No matter what we are being told or guided to from outside influences (no matter how good their intent), we must never forget to honor the internal guidance we receive from the voice within. The intuitive knowing we are born with has a connection to Universal Intelligence, God, Source Energy... *or whatever you feel most comfortable calling that power/force that connects all things.*

Somewhere along my journey, more than likely in childhood when my trust was violated and I was sexually molested, I began to lose that connection with myself, my knowing. That inner voice became harder and harder to hear. I didn't trust me. I didn't even know me. And I sought approval, answers, and guidance from outside sources to define who and what I was.

From the outside looking in, I was living the ideal life and had all the trappings of success. I'd graduated from high school at the age of sixteen, then went on to graduate from college by nineteen with two degrees, a major in arts and communication, and a minor in psychology. Being a highly effective communicator and understanding the human mind were always important subjects to me. The need to more fully understand this human experience, why we suffer, what we're here for, and how to get what we really want are questions that have always plagued my mind. So I searched.

By age twenty-one, I stepped into corporate America as the youngest district manager running a one-hundred and sixty million dollar technology sales business for one of the largest computer manufacturers in the world. I was following the societal script written for my life. Aren't you supposed to live the American dream? I had a company car, corporate spending accounts, a great salary, fantastic co-workers, and I traveled. Yes, there were plenty of challenges, but it was a GREAT LIFE, everything that one could ask for. Yet, I would still wake up feeling depressed, dragging myself out of bed, manufacturing a smile, and carrying on with my day like a puppet living in a lucid dream. What was wrong with me?

In the beginning, it was exciting, and it was new. It was everything I'd asked for and more. For four years of my decade tenure with the company, I even served as their National Spokesperson on television, representing and selling products on-air on major TV shopping channels.

What my accomplishments were doing was two-fold: on one side giving me invaluable experiences and knowledge, fulfilling my desires, and allowing me to taste that level of existence, while on the other hand serving as a distraction from my deeper work and purpose in life.

Think about it like a cross-country road trip. As you're driving, you'll have many stops along the way to see beautiful architecture, to take in the wonders of nature, maybe to walk along a breezy beach, fix a flat tire or two, eat ice cream at an old-fashioned diner, even visit friends and family to enjoy laughs and great conversation, but you aren't meant to stay at any one of those stops. They are but brief moments in time along a much bigger journey, and although there is a destination you've charted out, who you are becoming and what you are learning along the journey is the true prize of life.

This was only a part of my journey, but by no means had I reached the pinnacle of my purpose or potential. It was one stop along a much bigger path. The questions that pierced my mind in childhood still needed answers, and life refused to allow me to get stuck in this part of my journey because my real work had yet to begin.

THE LAYOFF

When we become complacent and refuse to listen to those internal nudges, sometimes God steps in. The company I had dedicated a decade of my life to sent out a department-wide email on a sunny July morning requesting we all attend a mandatory conference call that afternoon. The call was to inform us that due to a downturn in the economy, and uncertainty in business, we were all being laid off within the next two weeks. No one saw that coming! My entire existence and identity had become entangled with and defined by this job. Without the title and the trappings of success, I didn't know who I was. Have you ever felt so lost in your life?

Oddly enough, there was a part of me that was relieved. I had the opportunity to choose a different path, to go searching for answers, and figure out what I really wanted in life. Everyone around me, including my family, encouraged me to never leave that *"Good Job."* I didn't have the strength to do it on my own. People-pleasing had become all too common for me, and I had become quite comfortable in my discomfort. No one knew I was suffering. No one knew I'd reached the point of depression, feeling unfulfilled and yearning for something different. As I had done with many things in my life, I suffered in silence. Sometimes the seemingly worse situations, losses, even heartbreaks are really blessings in disguise. It took God, Universal Intelligence, Source Energy intervening to remove me from that job so that I could set out on the rest of my journey and make it to my next stop. When was the last time you felt the urge to make a significant change in your life in order to re-ignite your passion?

We all have so many gifts inside of us. Our lives, our journeys, our stories, our experiences, and our lessons learned are just as much for the development and advancement of humanity, and the collective conscious, as they are for us.

Like that cross-country road trip, my path has had so many stops *"Lifetime"* network could write a movie about it. From marriage and divorce to success and failure, and being broke and broken. Finding my voice, becoming an Author, and even breaking my silence of childhood sexual abuse. And if that wasn't enough,
I became a Queen (literally), set out on a new spiritual journey, and got lost along the way. I've reinvented myself, made history, and utilized my gifts in TV & Film. And like many of you, I've tragically lost loved ones in death, navigated natural disasters, a pandemic, and so much more.
But there is an important message in this for you! I feel compelled to share with you a divine manifesto I received and reveal the details of the journey that lead to that sacred channeled message. It contains life-altering implications and instructions for the voyage that you are currently embarking upon at this very moment!

THE JOURNEY BEGINS

We are weaving together this gigantic tapestry called life. Each piece and patch, whole within itself, yet interlocked with the next piece all revealing a bigger picture that is us, which is connected to the whole of all creation and everything in it.

Know that whatever you set your intention on and desire strongly is also seeking you. From childhood, I searched for answers, meaning, understanding, healing, fulfillment, connection, impact, and belonging. My journey has led to each of these things and more. For example, I serendipitously met a powerful woman who became a dear friend and confidant. I even crossed paths with a precarious young lady, under less than ideal circumstances, who became like a sister to me and my most trusted ally. Following those internal nudges and being thrust into new situations that held a piece of my puzzle led me to study under the mentorship of Tony Robbins, and even walking on fire! I have been introduced to life-changing tools like Neuro-Linguistic Programming (NLP), which allows you to re-wire your neural network and heal from trauma, enhance performance, and change behavioral patterns through specific linguistic commands delivered directly to your unconscious mind. Additionally, I've embraced other amazing techniques and practices such as Mental Emotional Release Therapy (MER), Neural Spinal Analysis (NSA), Hypnotherapy, Napoleon Hill's Principles of Success, 14 Universal Laws, 7 Hermetic Principles, Sacred Geometry, and Numerology to name a few.

These were things that I never knew existed. Some of which my former belief system and cultural upbringing would have dismissed, shunned, and told me were weird or wrong to pursue. There were many times in my journey I felt lost and alone, but my internal voice was always there. When I listened and allowed it to guide me, it continued to grow stronger and louder. I stepped into a place in my life where I was even able to break my silence about my childhood sexual abuse. I was no longer living in the shadow of the shame, guilt, and disgust I had for myself and my abuser. I began to love myself, to trust myself, and to help others do the same. I was finding my voice, speaking across the country, and making an impact. I was more fully unveiling my purpose, and yet the journey was far from over. There was still much work to be done. We are multidimensional beings. Once you've discovered and explored one layer, there are so many more to explore, to understand, to heal, to embrace, and to unleash.

I was led to one of my biggest life-changing experiences through a chance encounter that was by no means coincidental. The Universe is always orchestrating the alignment of certain pieces and people in our puzzle. I was booked to speak at a women's empowerment conference at a hotel in downtown New Orleans. After arriving at the venue, the event organizer led me down a hall towards the main ballroom where I was to speak. Along the hallway, there were sponsor and vendor tables set up displaying their goods and services. I was stopped for a brief interview by one of the event sponsors who was pre-recording episodes for "The Ladies Who" podcast. Upon finishing the interview, I headed into the ballroom to go on stage. After delivering my TED-style talk on "The Power of Enthusiasm," I was escorted to my book signing table, where I was met by one of the vendors who'd been in the ballroom during my speech. It was a gentleman by the name of Julian. He expressed how moved he was by the story I shared. He purchased both my books and began telling me about his own story. Realizing that we wouldn't have much time to talk, he took one of my business cards and said he would reach out and connect later. However, as with most things, life happens and "later" slips further and further away, into never.

To my surprise, a year after the conference, I received an unexpected call from Julian. We exchanged some niceties, and then he got right down to business requesting a lunch meeting. We set the time and location, and within a week, we were sitting across from each other nibbling on hush puppies and crab au gratin at his family's seafood restaurant. But something extremely odd happened, as if a switch had been flipped. What started out as a strictly business luncheon turned extremely personal and highly spiritual. A door had been opened, revealing a path to information that couldn't have come at a better time. I thought I was there to bring on a new client or be introduced to a new speaking opportunity. Yet, a much deeper, much more important assignment was being laid out.

Julian shared that he was embarking upon a journey to sit with a Shaman in a sacred plant ceremony with Ayahuasca in the next three weeks. My ears perked up, and my heart began to soar. I had heard of Ayahuasca and had even studied up on this South American brew used as a spiritual medicine made from two sacred plants in the Amazon rainforest. But I'd never had the courage to actually try it myself. And here this person was sitting in front of me who was about to partake in the ancient ritual that I felt so called to but was too afraid to actually do. Everyone who I had previously spoken to about it had pre-judged it as being "way too out there." Or those who had done it seemed to lead a lifestyle that didn't feel in alignment with me, so whatever they were doing, I wanted no part of. It's like going to a beauty salon or barbershop seeking a stylist only to find that the floor is dirty. The chair is full of hair. The tools haven't been cleaned in God knows how long. Oh, and the shop owner's hair looks a HOT mess. No, ma'am. No thank you. I'll pass. Although they may have had valid information about Ayahuasca, as a student, I was not ready or willing to learn from a teacher who did not feel like a good fit.

It is very true that when the student is ready, the teacher will appear. We will find the messenger who resonates with us through word, deed, and experience. And Julian was the right one to deliver the message and open the door to me about Ayahuasca when I was ready to receive it. Although he hadn't even had his own experience yet, I was able to join the journey nearly from the beginning as an observer and explore through him. We set a follow-up meeting for his return after his ceremony, so I could hear every detail, gain a better understanding of his experience, and determine if this was the right path for me.

DECISION TIME

Nearly a month had passed, Julian was back, and I was extremely excited. We met for lunch at a nearby Whole Foods. He was still on a special post-ceremony diet to keep his mind and body purified for the insights and integration that were still to come. Apparently, prior to the ceremony, you are given a special diet to prepare the body for the experience, and immediately following the ceremony, you continue on a slightly modified diet as you begin to slowly incorporate foods back into your normal eating patterns. The mind, body, and spirit are all connected and work in harmony with each other. So, to have the most heightened spiritual experience, our body must be on board, along with the mind, as they are both sacred and important pieces of the whole.

As we sat down after making our selections from the freshly prepared food bar, I noticed a lot of veggies, plain white fish, and sweet potatoes on Julian's plate. Foods I would consider boring but definitely healthy, to say the least. Like an eager puppy who could barely contain itself, my mind ran wild with curiosity in anticipation of what Julian would say. I wanted no stone unturned, and no detail missed. I was ready to soak in every ounce of his experience as if it were my own. I listened intently as he spoke, and through his description, I was able to envision every corner of the room, the vibration of the melodious chants bellowed out by the Shaman, and the woodsy taste of the dark bitter brew he drank. His words gave me a glimpse into every unfolding encounter during his tale and the brilliant light at the end of the tunnel that led to his own personal healing and insights.

It was like nothing I had heard before, and I was enchanted. I was now ready to face my own dark places and insecurities and experience my own light through this reverentially vulnerable experience. I urged Julian to call the ceremony coordinator and make an introduction right then and there. That's when I met Rhonda, whom I now refer to as the fairy godmother of the cosmic family. Her warmth could be felt through the phone. She shared insights and helped provide a level of comfort that made it easy for me to say yes. I'd found my tribe and network of support for this next stop on my journey of growth, and I'd identified a tool and process that would lead me there. In less than three months, I would be embarking upon my very own Ayahuasca ceremony.

I was ready, and I was scared as hell! So many things ran through my mind in the days and weeks leading up to my trip. What would my family think? Is this truly safe? I'd watched documentaries about people undergoing these ceremonies and having a wide spectrum of experiences from pissing and shitting on themselves as they purged dark energy from their body to experiencing beautiful psychedelic images, deep psychic healing of childhood wounds, and even recovering from physical ailments and pain. I wanted none of the shitting and pissing experience, but all of the healing! And I had no idea what was in store for me, so I had to trust my internal guidance, knowing I made the right decision. I researched as much as possible and allowed Rhonda and her sacred community to show me the way. I even found that Ayahuasca, which is also called Grandmother, consists of a spiritual energy that begins to work with you long before taking a sip of her bitter brew in ceremony. Both philosophers Ralph Waldo Emerson and physicist Albert Einstein agreed on this one fact, "All is energy." Einstein adding, "Energy cannot be created or destroyed. It can only be changed from one form to another."

SURRENDER

In preparation for the ceremony, Rhonda provided us with reading material like Javier Regueiro's book *"Ayahuasca"* to equip our minds, a special Shamanic diet to purify our bodies, and community Zoom calls with participants around the world to answer questions and alleviate confusion and fear. It was quite comforting and exactly what I needed in order to keep taking each next step on my path.

What I found was that insights, information, and breakthroughs started coming to me and happening through me long before I went into the ceremony. The energy of transformation was already at work as I was learning to surrender and let go. From everything that I had read, the only way for me to get the most out of my experience with Ayahuasca was for me to surrender, but I was such a control freak. I attempted to keep all factors within my grasp because, for the vast majority of my life, I felt so out of control, especially during the time that I was sexually abused as a child. So, throughout my adulthood, I overcompensated by trying to be in control of everything. It was a safety mechanism, which I also knew was a key element holding me back from reaching my full potential. And on a deeper level, control is such an illusion. The only thing we can truly control is our own mind and the way we choose to interpret and react to the things that happen. So, this was an area of real struggle for me, to let go of my illusion. I wanted everything that Grandmother Ayahuasca was ready to reveal to me, so I had to find a way to let go and allow her to take the wheel.

One day while taking a walk, I began contemplating what it truly meant to surrender, and a vision came to me. It was like God downloaded this movie straight into my brain, and I watched each scene play out as clear as day. Whether you call it channeling, or clairvoyance, or a divine download, it was a very powerful experience, and this new insight drastically shifted my perspective. I pulled out my phone, and as quickly as I could, I captured in words everything that I had seen in my mind's eye. This was what I saw:

A Vision of Surrender (Death of the Ego)

"Today I sat beside a tree
and an eagle swallowed me whole.
I surrendered to its grasp,
then a snake swallowed us both.

All three descending into abyss.
Deep within the core of the earth,
grounded in its glory.
The energy circulating,
protecting us as we were being molded.

The snake ascended.
We were renewed.
It released us from its belly, and then we flew.
High, so high beyond the sky.

I then burst forth from the eagle's beak,
holding within me the reverence of the sea.
And the illumination of the stars.
Bold, with the force of the Phoenix,
reminding us of who we are.

With one last look at creation,
I merged with all that is.
Becoming one with the Divine,
in accord with my Purpose."

This vision helped me tremendously. I finally let go, and this was only the start of many powerful visions to come. We are all born with the ability to connect with divine energy and information. Yet, due to our own earthly experiences, societal teachings, and personal beliefs, we often block our ability to connect. Surrendering is an ongoing practice. I've found that there are levels to letting go, as there are levels to all things. As in spiral dynamics, as you go higher and deeper in understanding, there is always more to learn, more to explore, and more to apply in every aspect of our lives. I was attracting people and experiences that were testing me and revealing areas I needed to work on, including money blocks, lack of patience, my relationship with anger, and my sense of worthiness to attain my deepest desires. The time was getting closer for me to drink in the wise counsel of Grandmother Ayahuasca, and I was ready.

The day I had so anxiously awaited had finally arrived, and my intentions were set for what I wanted to gain from this experience. I wanted to become more at one with myself. I yearned to trust myself and my intuition more. I needed to see the truth and fully understand what I am. I longed for help in becoming more compassionate, patient, and understanding of others. I also wanted to see and experience the extent of our human potential and know what the grand plan for life really is. I desired to know how to access all of my power and more extensively use it for good. And, last but not least, I wanted to clearly understand and see my next steps and summon the courage to do it, whatever "it" may be.

THE AYAHUASCA EXPERIENCE

Upon arriving at the retreat center, I was greeted by familiar faces I'd seen on so many Zoom calls prior. It felt like a reunion of old friends meeting for the first time in person. So, there was a level of comfort walking into this new environment that, over the next five days, we would bond in while simultaneously going on our own deep individual journey of healing and discovery with Ayahuasca.

We sat comfortably in a large circle in the spacious living room, our attention laser-focused on each other as we went from person to person, candidly sharing our intentions for being there and what we hoped to gain. Many in the circle were veterans of the process, having previously attended several Ayahuasca ceremonies.

I was one of the newbies and felt some level of relief knowing they had not only survived the experience but found it beneficial enough to return for even deeper insights. During our circle of sharing, Sal, one of the event facilitators, offered some additional medicinal tools to enhance the Ayahuasca journey. One of which was rapé, a sacred cleansing tobacco from the Amazon administered up the nasal cavity with a pipe. It is used to clear bad energy and focus and sharpen the mind. As well as the tropical plant sananga, which is administered as an eye drop to help expand vision and spiritual awareness during the ceremony. The rapé burned and sananga stung, but I had come this far and wanted the full experience, so I was all in!

One by one, we were led outside into a massive teepee to meet the Shaman, and be cleansed with tobacco and Florida water for protection. Prayers were also recited to call in our ancestors and spiritual guides to help us and remove any entities that may try to impede our journey. The Shaman wasn't anything like I'd imagined. First of all, I thought *she* would be a *he*. Every documentary I had watched always showed the Shaman as either a super-thin older man who was fully shaved or a robust man with a long thick wiry beard. This apparently is a huge misconception since some of the most powerful Shamanic practitioners across indigenous cultures are women. This woman was unique indeed. She had a very cool gothic vibe going on. She reminded me of Abby, the forensic scientist from the NCIS TV series. I really was not prepared for how modern and mystic yet super approachable she was. It created a whole new paradigm in my mind of what was possible. That is why we should never put people in boxes, judging who or what they are, or even what they could become based on outdated stereotypes. That was my first lesson of the night, and oh boy, was I in for some major lessons well above and beyond this!

The ceremony room was pretty much an open space lined with comforters and plush mats, along with pillows and blankets arranged for each participant around three of the four walls, with large windows embedded in two of them that offered a dreamy view of the dark night sky. The fourth wall at the head of the room was where the Shaman and her assistant sat, ready to guide our ceremony and dispense the sacred brew we had all come to consume. Next to each of our mats was a bright orange bucket, yup, you guessed it, for convenient access in case we needed to vomit, a common aspect of the Ayahuasca experience for many. It is often symbolic of releasing blockages or purging that which no longer serves you so that you can go deeper into your healing work. Prior to arriving, one of my greatest fears was that I would be one of the lucky participants who would piss and shit on themselves during the ceremony, so I took a little preemptive action. I generously lined my underwear with so many super-absorbent maxi pads that I was pretty much wearing an adult diaper (just in case). I wasn't leaving that to chance!

As we prepared for what was to be a life-changing night, Rhonda began passing a bag of crystals around the room, with each person being allowed to take one they felt connected or called to. Crystals create great vibrational flow, and I was looking for all the good vibes I could get. So, I graciously dug deep inside and, upon feeling the one, took it and passed the bag along. Next came around a drawstring bag filled with salt, which we each took a pinch of, stated our intentions in an almost prayer-like meditation out loud, and then released the salt and our intentions to the Universe. I listened to each person's entreaty with great admiration for their courageousness to take this path, knowing that not too long from that very moment, we would all be deeply immersed in a sea of infinite experiences uniquely our own. Not two of us seeing, feeling, or encountering the exact same thing, but embarking upon individual expeditions into the unknown, trusting that the path would lead us to what we needed most.

The lights were lowered, and one by one, we were directed up to the Shaman to sip in the wisdom of Grandmother Ayahuasca, and what only seemed like a shot glass full of brew tasted like the bark of a million trees planted in the deepest depths of the Amazon forest. The mixture was dark, thick, and murky. Each of my taste buds were being fully submerged by the dense gulp. It had a very unpleasant bite, but I welcomed the discomfort because I was more interested in the benefits that were to come. The Shaman further instructed us to gauge how we were feeling, and within thirty minutes, she would call for another round of Ayahuasca. She added that if we could ask ourselves if we needed another cup, that was a clear sign that we definitely needed another cup and to make our way up to the front to receive it. Upon taking my second bitter gulp of brew, I slowly crawled back to my mat, and deep down the rabbit hole, I went. I could hear the melodious sounds of beautiful icaros belting forth from the Shaman's lips. Icaros are traditional indigenous songs, or musical prayers and chants, that embody the spirit and power of the plant and help to guide the healing journey. On that dark starry night, like a shepherd guiding her flock through the pasture, the icaros warmly bid me to embrace the kaleidoscope of colors and patterns I saw emerging in the room. I felt a tingle flow through me like an ocean wave as the weight of my extremities compounded. It was time to surrender. I let go and dived deeply inward into my impenetrable places as my body lay limp on the mat. There I saw many visions and underwent a great deal of unfathomable experiences.

MERRY-GO-ROUND

I found myself completely enthralled on a lavishly whimsical carousel ride, as the centrifugal force spun me round and round. I leaned back and let out a shrill of excitement as my hands tightly grasped the pole going up and down atop a cheerfully painted horse with elaborate gold trim. The smile on my face beaming from ear to ear as the familiar circus-like tune played vibrantly in the air, intensifying the fun and exhilaration with each spin. Again and again, I went round and round, feeling the joyous control I had over my life, over the moment, everything spinning in its rightful place. But something went wrong. What was wondrous and beautiful came to a jarring halt and morphed into a nightmare. Figures of thick stocky men in fedoras and black-and-white pinstripe suits appeared sporting devilish grins, feverishly laughing in between puffs of their cigars. Stop it. Why can't I make this stop? This was no merry-go-round, and there was nothing merry about this. I was stuck on this never-ending loop going round and round. Their laughter was growing louder. The manipulating look in their eyes was as if they controlled the world, the stock markets, the media, and the decisions we make on a daily basis. They kept standing there mocking me with their laughter. Why can't I get off this ride? I can do this. I can make this stop. Then momentary relief came as the figures vanished. Okay, I got this, take that you old geezers! Who's in control now? Oh shit, wait, it's starting up again, they are back, and I can't get off this God-forsaken ride. The cycle keeps repeating itself over and over and over again, countless times. At this point, I'm flat-out tired and so over this Ayahuasca shit. I am ready to come out of this, but I can't. So I finally implored Grandmother Ayahuasca for help, and she revealed the way out.

One of the aspects of preparation for our ceremony was partaking in a very specific and somewhat strict diet that would help cleanse the body. I enthusiastically embraced this challenge and even took it a step further by fasting for a period of time. I was so proud of myself, but as the date got closer, my old yet familiar frenemy "self-sabotage" reared its ugly head. At the airport, I walked into the bakery and ordered a breakfast sandwich and items from the menu that were not aligned with the diet we were instructed to follow.

I rationalized with myself that I had done such a great job prior that it was okay to break this one little rule. I convinced myself I wasn't hurting anybody, and who would know anyway.

In the very moment that I asked for help to break free from that nightmarish carousel ride, the memory of this incident came flooding into my mind. I realized that those bloated Al Capone type figures were held in place by lies. They were a mirror of the lies I was telling myself. A reflection of the pain I had inflicted on myself when I thought I wasn't hurting anybody. I had turned a blind eye to my self-sabotaging behavior and justified years of abuse through negative self-talk, harmful eating patterns, hatred, and guilt. Our greatest responsibility is to love ourselves. How can you love your neighbor as yourself if you don't know how to truly love yourself? I am somebody too. I am responsible to myself, to be honest, to be loving, and to be fair to me. This awareness was such a gift, and it freed me from the maniacal merry-go-round. I was thrust forward like a quantum leap into a universal experience beyond space and time. What came next was truly mind-blowing.

THE MULTIVERSE

I was engulfed in vast openness, very reminiscent of outer space, surrounded in darkness but with the ability to see a concave of blue waves around me. Where was I? What was I experiencing? I felt as if I was suffocating, my throat depleted of oxygen. How would I breathe? Then one breath of life deeply inhaled, was all that was there, and it was all that was needed. This one breath appeared in the form of a magnificent blue water droplet. With this one breath, so many forms of life alchemically emerged. I was witnessing the creation of life itself. Not just witnessing it, I was experiencing it. It was so beautiful and awe-inspiring, yet the very visceral feeling of intense pressure in my throat from the nanoscopic amount of air used in this process did not escape my notice. The beginning of the cycle of life starts with one breath, then bubbles, the formless turned into form, darkness into light, then a distinct popping sound could be heard. The creation of life not just on our planet or in our Universe, but across the Multiverse! We are not alone.

A VESSEL

After this extraordinary universal experience of creation, my awareness was brought back into my physical body in the ceremony room as I lay on my mat. However, my body was not my own. I mean, it was my body, and I keenly felt everything that was happening, but the experience I was now undergoing was not mine. I felt the exhaustion of being chased in dark woods through murky swamps. My body was adorned in a tattered white dress, filthy and wet with my hair tied up in a burlap scarf. This had never happened to me personally, but I felt it as if it had. My body began to convulse with the pain of rape and physical assault, but this was not my own. At first, I did not know what was happening or why this was happening. But I began to realize I was being used as a vessel. These horrific things had not happened to me but to our ancestors. Africans, Indigenous tribes, Native Americans, Jews, and so many more, I felt them all. I felt the slaughter, the abuse, all the horrifying mistreatment by the hands of man as my body unceasingly writhed on the floor of the ceremony room. Tears streaming down my face as wave after wave of these experiences swept through me. I wanted it to stop, but this wasn't even about me anymore. For years I'd declared, "Here I Am. Send Me," offering my life up to Universal Intelligence to use for a purpose greater than myself. That knowing fortified me as this experience persisted on. The Shaman, undoubtedly perceiving my struggle, aided me with a euphoric chant, and puffs of sacred tobacco wafted over my body with a feathered fan, which began to soothe my restlessness.

Then came the gift in the tribulation. My body began preparing itself for birth. I wasn't pregnant, yet I felt life in my belly. My breathing pattern changed. I began sipping in deep breaths as if getting ready to push. My legs propped open ready to release something monumental. I pushed, and I pushed, and I felt the release of new life. It was more than an individual or a baby, it was Universal life being brought forth, a Universe of change that came through me, and I was the vessel.

THE NIGHT SKY

I was now more conscious of the space I was in and my surroundings, more alert, and back to being me in my own body. Everyone still in the ceremony room was in some stage of their own experience, while others had already left the room. I had no concept of time and wasn't even aware that so many hours had already passed. I started to feel the need to use the restroom, but as I attempted to move realized my legs were not sturdy, and I felt very spaced-out. Standing up was not an option, so I slowly began crawling towards the door. As I staggered across the floor, I noticed there were planetary star stickers on the ground that glowed in the dark to help direct our path forward. A memory flashed in my mind from earlier that evening of the Shaman's assistant pointing a flashlight down at the floor. I wasn't fully paying attention to what she was doing because the Shaman was sharing some words of wisdom. Now, with this heightened sense of awareness, that moment came back to me. She was apparently activating the stickers with her flashlight. And indeed, they shined brightly. There were moments I became so captivated by the stars, staring so closely in amazement, that my face was practically touching the floor. They certainly helped me make my way across the room, although my intense fascination with the stars significantly prolonged the trek. As I finally approached the door, I tried to stand up again, but my balance was still off. Evidently, seeing my dilemma, Sal, one of the practitioners, rushed over to assist me and lend a hand. He was so gentle and reassuring. He guided me to the restroom and stood outside the door, periodically asking if I was okay. I must have spent a long time in that bathroom.

Thankfully my precautionary pads were not needed. I made it to the restroom and had a very relieving and gratifying pee (no poop). But I kept getting off the toilet and then asking myself, am I done? And then I would sit back down, and a couple more drops of pee would come out. I think I did this 20 times (I'm sure it wasn't, but it felt like it). Then I was struck with the overwhelming urge to puke, which I must have said audibly because Sal asked if I needed a bucket and then graciously brought me one. I stared deep down into the depths of that bucket, wondering if I had something to contribute in the way of contents. Moments later, like a river of darkness, I saw gobs of dark energy spewing forth from my mouth into the bucket. Wave after wave, I purged physically and spiritually. The gut-wrenching projectile release was so surreal. I felt a sense of massive relief.

Sal guided me out of the bathroom and gently placed a small glass of cool water in my hand to sip on while he disposed of the contents of the bucket.

Feeling ready to move again, I leaned into Sal's arm as he escorted me back towards the room. As we came near the sliding door adjacent to the patio, I expressed interest in going outside instead. Upon opening the door, the cool brisk air whisked past my face with a rush of vitality. This was exactly where I was supposed to be, partaking in this fresh, invigorating air outside. I was guided to a chair on the lawn as I watched fellow ceremony participants in various phases of their journey. Some walking about the grass, others laid out in lawn chairs, and a few conversing quietly in a corner. Although they were whispering, I could hear them so loudly and kept thinking to myself that I wish I had a mute button. This just felt like a moment for silent contemplation of this profound experience.

I felt the warmth of a thick, cozy blanket being placed over me, shielding me from the crisp night breeze. After expressing my immense gratitude, my gaze tilted upward towards the starry sky above. There was something very distinct in the firmament. The sky was covered with intersecting horizontal and vertical lines emitting a bluish-white light. I wondered if anyone else could see this magnetic grid that appeared as if cast over the sky by a fisherman's net in perfectly proportioned squares with brilliantly illuminated stars seen clearly on the other side. It felt like it was a protective barrier of some kind. But to protect us from what? And why had I never seen this before? I sat staring in amazement at this natural phenomenon I had the privilege of observing that night. As I began to feel the heaviness of my eyelids ushering on the welcome relaxation of sleep, I asked for assistance to return to my mat and nodded off comfortably across my pillow.

THE DIVINE DOWNLOAD

I sprung out of bed as if a cock crowed, sounding the alarm it was time to rise and shine. I am typically not an early morning person, but my body clock deemed it necessary that I awaken. There was something yearning to come out of me. This time it wasn't any bodily fluids but a message instead. The night prior, as we were setting intentions for our ceremony, one of the things I asked for was to have the ability to understand the grand plan of life, see my next steps, and access the courage to do it. So I put a pen and notebook under my mat just in case I was inspired to capture any insights that came forth. The time had come, and I felt compelled to write, so I stood up and walked into the sunroom, found a nice cozy spot, and settled in.

A ray of light caught my attention as it cascaded through the room. I was struck with a deep sense of awe watching as the sun pirouetted across the glass, through the window, and glistened off the still water of the pool. I sat engulfed in every detail of the moment. A tear gradually descended from my eye and softly flowed down the side of my cheek. Everything moved in slow motion as I followed the wind rustling through the branches of the trees. It was all so magical. There was a lifetime in those moments that I humbly inhaled through my eyes and every pore of my being. My head tilted down towards my notebook, my pen converged upon the paper, and as if in a trance, I wrote page after page after page until the delivery of the message was complete, and I was released.

During the time I was receiving this divinely inspired message, a couple of the retreat participants came into the room. One young lady tried engaging in conversation with me, but I was unable to utter a single word. I lifted my head up, offering her a brief nod of acknowledgment, and then back to writing, my hand returned.

Inexplicably, she graciously honored the process and state that I was in and left me in peace to complete my assignment. Once the final word was laid to paper, as if awakened from a lucid dream, I was totally back to being my talkative, gregarious self, engaging with others, inquiring what they were up to, and ready to eat breakfast. I was hungry!

If you have made it this far, it's because you possess a spiritual hunger and a significant purpose in life that must be fulfilled. The divine manifesto that I channeled was not just for me but for you too, to be used as a guide to help you along your path. This sacred prayer will help unveil your next steps in this great journey called life and deliver a message of hope during these times of significant change.

A Divine Manifesto

WE ARE RE-WRITING A NEW HISTORY.

All the content of the Universe is contained

in a single drop of water.

Water cleanses.

Water purifies.

Water reveals truth.

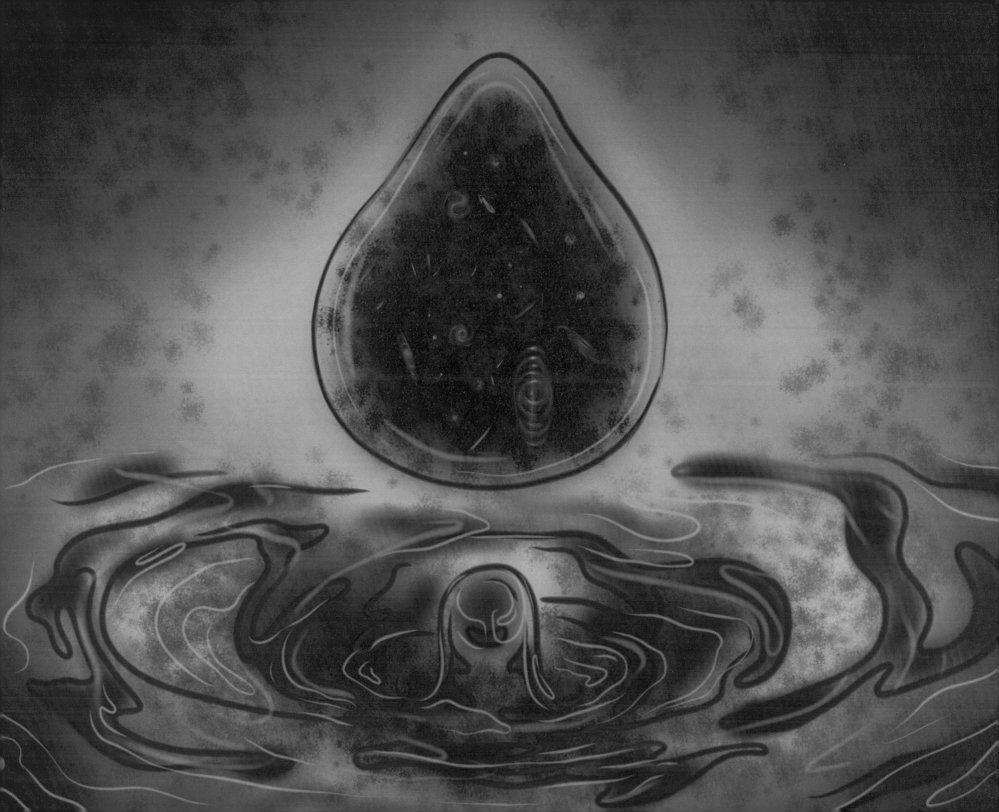

The truth is,

we have not been very good stewards of our resources,
our powers,
our gifts,
our voices,
our bodies,
our earth,
our minds,
our intentions,
our truth.
Clouded, distorted, manipulated, abused, suppressed, misused, mistreated.

We are dying.

But with death brings with it the gift of a new birth.

Our system of things is passing away and so are its desires.

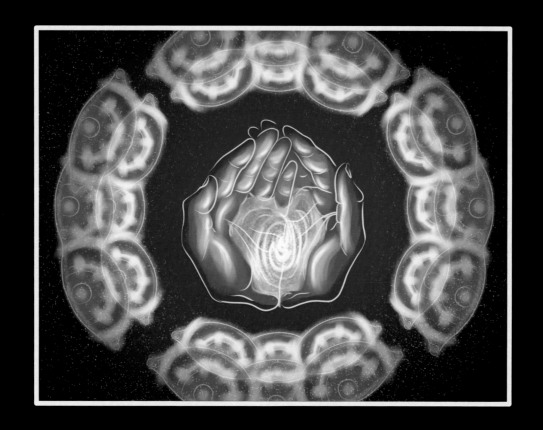

We are bringing forth a new intention,
a new harmony for and with life,
a new Multiverse as never seen, felt, imagined
or experienced before.

CALLING UPON EVERY DIMENSION

KNOWN AND UNKNOWN,

every power known and unknown.

Birthing new elements,

new formulas,

new beings of infinite light and capacity.

Our Ancestors

have heard our cries
and they cry with us and through us,
their pain is felt and heard
throughout the cosmos.

One breath which brings forth life.
One breath held, which restricts life.

Breathe.

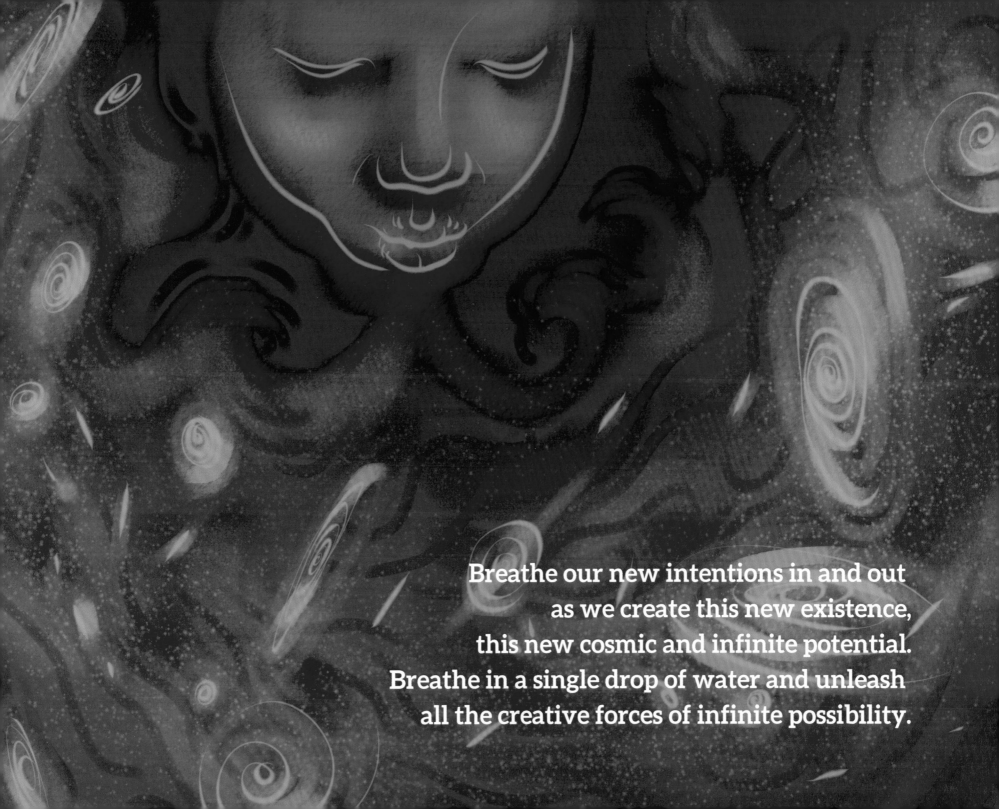

Breathe our new intentions in and out
as we create this new existence,
this new cosmic and infinite potential.
Breathe in a single drop of water and unleash
all the creative forces of infinite possibility.

We, Our Generation

with the help of our precious ancestral lineages,
traditions known and forgotten, known and unknown
are converging on the leading edge of a new birth.

For all atrocities held in our cosmic and physical
cellular memory are being transmuted into

Light, Love, and New Creation.

Every murder, countless millennia of rape, of hatred, of ignorance,
of pain, of love unrequited, of silence, of slavery, of suppression,
of lies masked and cloaked as truth, are now being given voice,
expression, release, justice, peace, cleansing, unfolding, washing away.

For a new generation unlike any before it.
Who were / are born to remember
why we came here,
our purpose, the cosmic joke.
The ability to transcend karma,
rising to a new plane of consciousness,
one in which we remember and live in our connection to all things.

One where peace abounds.

Where ancestors dance their
melodious tunes onto the fabric of this
New Universe.

Where all possibility exists not as a seed within us but as the ripe, blossoming tree of life flowering and seeding simultaneously.

Transcendence will be the way of life,
not the extraordinary, unreachable,
ions of work we have made it to be.
In the silence we hear all,
we feel all, we know all.
In our connection we experience all.

We Are One.

Today, right now in this moment choose.

Choose to break the cycle of lies that you once told yourself.

Today, choose to live in truth.
Today, choose to live in unconditional love.
Today, choose to see the light.
Today, choose to face the dark.
Today, choose to transmit your true intent,
your absolute and ever evolving truth to the
infinite vast unbounded moldable fabric of the Universe.
Give and Receive.
Love and Be Loved.

Free Yourself.
You are a human and infinite revolution.
No longer be silenced.
You are free if you allow yourself to be.

I saw and experienced
everything and nothing short of miraculous.
I saw the cycles,
the head games we play with ourselves.
The lies we accept, the lies we tell.
The truth and light we suppress.
The abuse we inflict on ourselves and each other,
which just ripples back to our own fabric and makeup.

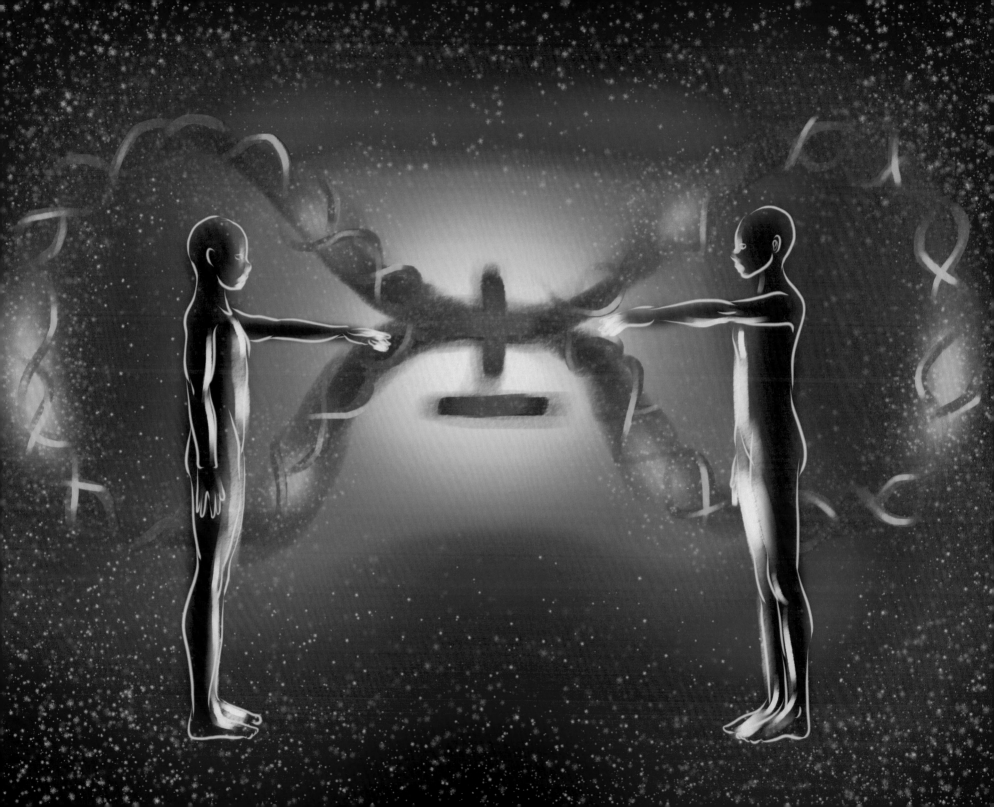

I AM SO SORRY

for not honoring this amazing gift of life.
This privilege to be a vessel
for transmuting and translating truth.
I am a powerful being
with the power to create and birth Universes,
new Multiverses.

With the power is a vessel
to hear and heal lineages of
all people, tribes, tongues,
seen and unseen,
known and unknown.

They all flowed through me,
they all live within me.
And I live within all of you.

We are bound to the end of time which is never.
There is no end of time because time only
exists within certain dimensions,
and there are more dimensions than the
finite mind can imagine or even count.

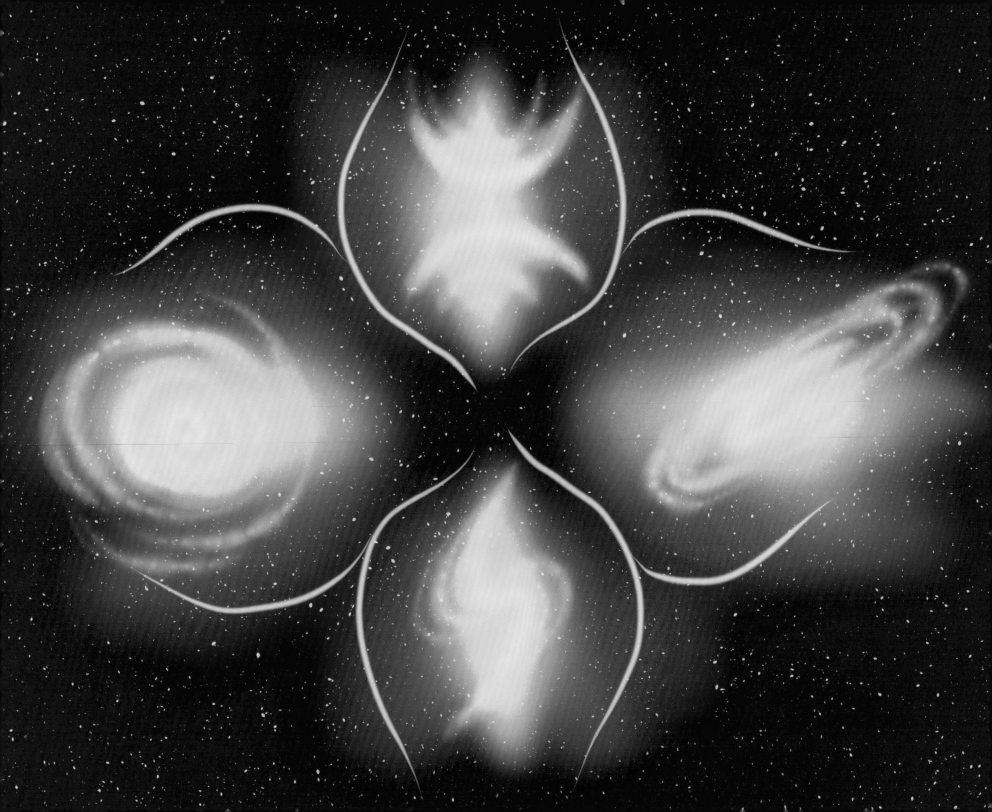

Seven dimensions ha!
Nine dimensions that's a joke,
a far cry from the innumerable,
infinite layers of existence.
Nineteen, forty, no there are more,
many many more.

Each with its own signature,
its own ecosystem,
each with its own experience of itself.

There is not one source of power,
ALL IS POWER.
All cannot be explained
only experienced.

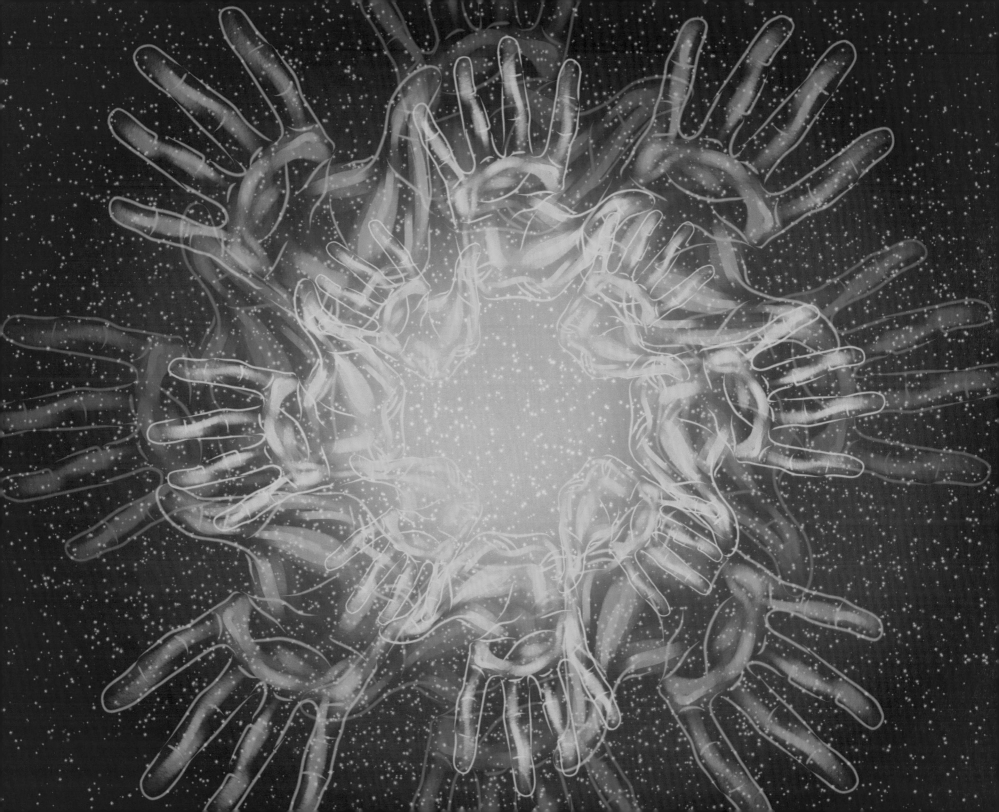

We must trust our infinite reach into the dark vast unknown.

Trust that we are light, illuminating the way,

creating and unveiling the roadmap.

We are the force,

the intention,

the creators of our existence in connection with ALL.

All is a vibration,

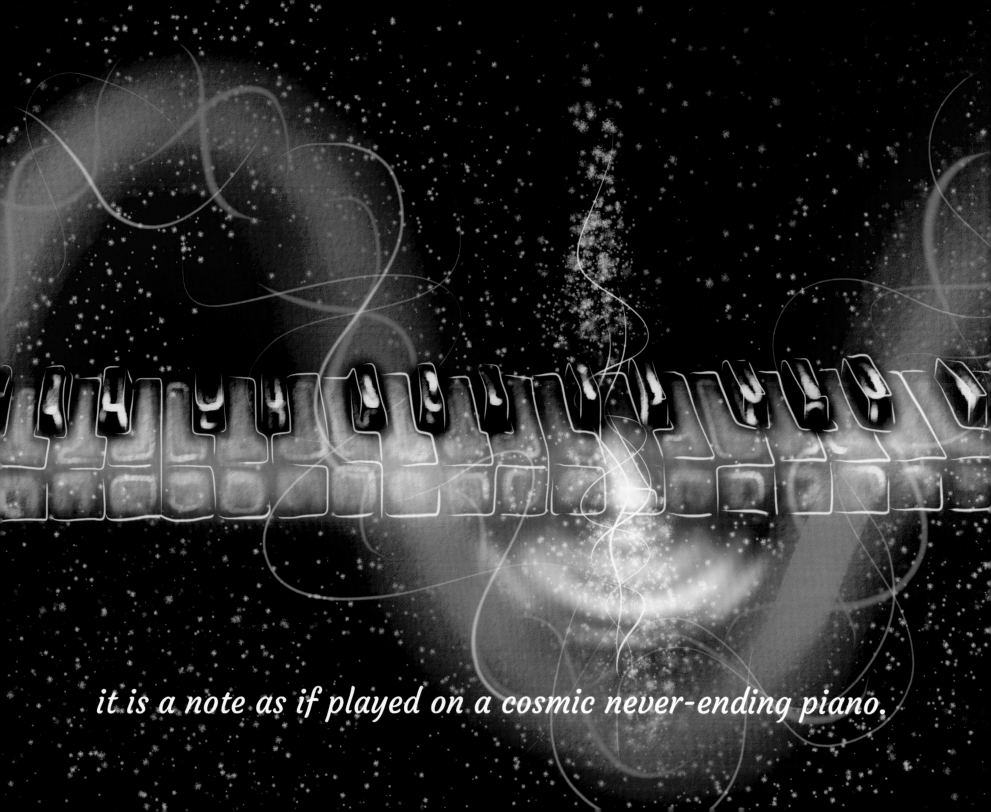

it is a note as if played on a cosmic never-ending piano.

These words do not express
the depth and breadth of what
I wish to share with you.
It must be invited in,
given permission.
The experience of All,
it must be granted access.
You must say yes to see, feel,
exhort, and habitate with All.

We have so easily given our power away
to flashy illusions.
Things that we created.
Figments of our imagination.

We birthed them,
then we worshipped them,
as if they had life outside of us.
.

It is All in Us.

It is better to worship nothing.
It is better to exalt nothing.
It is better to bless all.
It is better to breathe all.
It is better to drink in the simple,
unwavering truth of all.

Gratitude not reverence.
Love not worship.
We worship sand and wind,
What the hell or heaven are we doing?
We have forgotten.

But All is Well.

One breath creates new life.

We / I am calling upon,
calling in ALL for the creation
of a new system of things,
a new Multiverse is birthed.

It is our job to adjust our frequency, our knowing
to this new place which exists in this place,
in place, not in space and time,
but in knowing,
allowing,
experiencing.

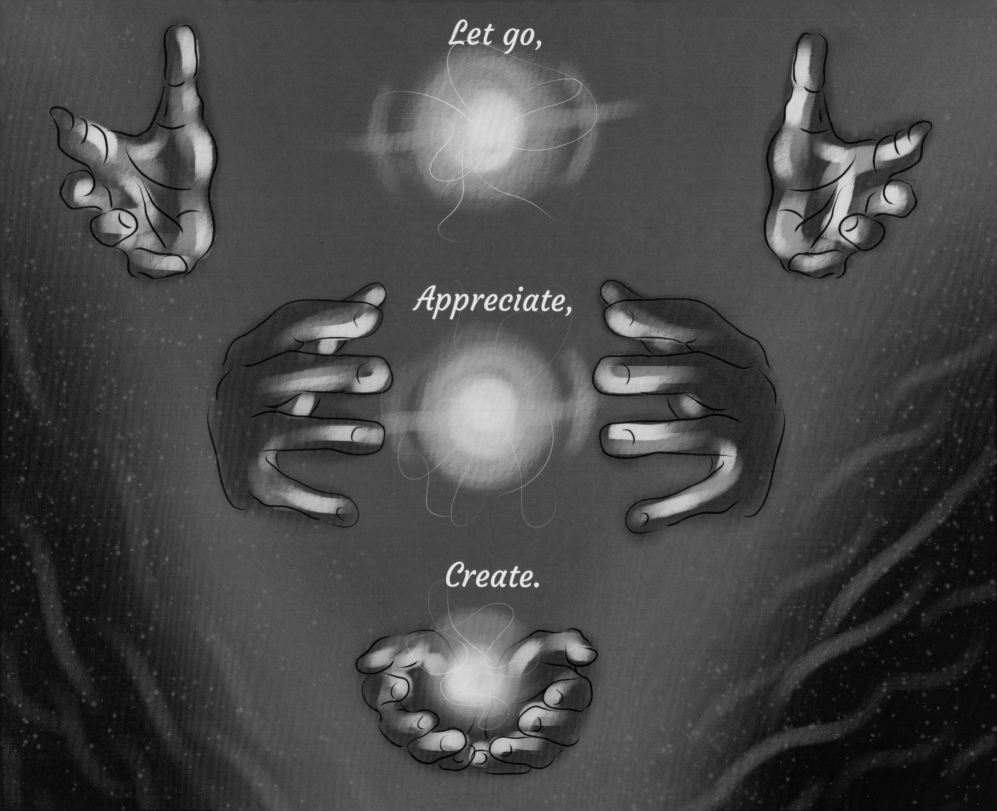

That is the story of Life.

Now I did see some pretty cool sh*t on this trip.

A trip indicates going somewhere,
and maybe it is somewhere,
no where,
in where,
out where,
Where?

That's not really important.
Actually there are not too many things
that are "important".
We have given
so much,
too much,
and not enough power away.

Instead of ingesting our power and
creating angels (light),
we've created demons (darkness)
— not to be confused with dark matter
that is used in the fabric of creation,
but the darkness of forgetting,
the darkness of fear.

The dark matter that exists in the
Universe is pure potentiality awaiting
instruction on what we want molded
into and out of it.
It is the purest essence of being.
There is so much intelligence
and power,
pure positive power just awaiting our
command to become anything
we set our intentions on.

And we have wielded that power
unjustly, unmercifully
to our own detriment.
But life will always find a way to
cleanse, purify, call, and support that
which supports more of itself.
It will neither be destroyed or denied
its pure expression of love.
That is why a new Multiverse
is being / is birthed.
Life will never be the same.

You have Awakened,
you have felt my great power,
my great love,
my sense of purpose,
my sense of joy, my joke,
and my vast being.

Go forth, cleanse and purify your vessel.

Stay connected to me.

I am always whispering in your ear,

Always here to guide you

when you allow me.

I will always support you,

show you your way, the way.

There are many many ways,

don't ever get too stuck on any one path.

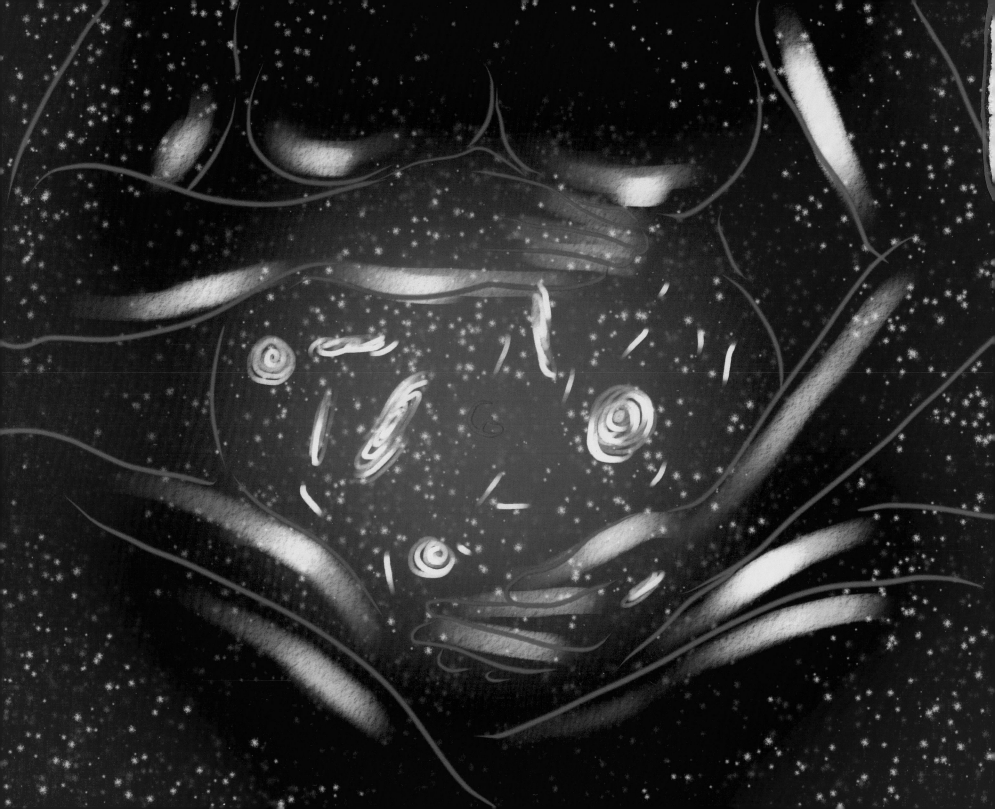

I flow, I am flexible,
I move, I breathe, I exhale life.
My womb births Nations and Universes.

It will never be fully understood
with the finite mind,
so join me in the infinite mind.
And I will freely and lovingly, gently,
and forcefully if you are ready,
Show you Everything.

Time is of no consequence,
it all exists in this moment.
So fret not that it will all get done.
It will and it will never stop unfolding.

Enjoy the trip, the journey, the path
for it is unending and ever present.

I AM ALWAYS WITH YOU.
CALL UPON ME
AND KNOW THAT I AM ALL.

Epilogue

WHERE DO WE GO FROM HERE?

We are the generation that is rewriting a new history. The choices we make today determine the direction of our lives and the direction of the new world. For me, The Divine Manifesto was a much needed wake up call to start deliberately living my life on purpose. We were born to SHINE, and that is exactly what I plan to do. The insights I gained inspired me to develop a formula I could live by:

S - Stop Settling
H - Heal Internally
I - Ignite Your Passion
N - Network with Winners
E - Empower Others

This simple 5 Step Formula helped me re-evaluate my course of action, implement wisdom gained, unleash my full potential, and put myself in a position to Be Proof Of What's Possible!

Stop Settling

"You must feed your mind with reading material, thoughts, and ideas that open you to new possibilities," expressed media mogul and philanthropist Oprah Winfrey.

When looking back on your life, you begin to see the string that connects every road you've ever taken and exactly where it has led. I realized I had been incorporating these steps long ago, which led me to this very point in my life. I had to stop settling for the narrative I'd adopted in childhood of life having limited possibilities. It is essential that we expand our vision by studying the lives and stories of those who have come before us. One thing about success is that it leaves clues. Read books, take courses, and ask for help. We are not alone in the obstacles and challenges we face. If others could overcome them, so can we!

Heal Internally

Once you know what's possible for your life, then you can heal internally and become the person you've always wanted to be. As mentioned earlier, I have embraced many healing modalities that have aided me throughout my journey, such as NLP, MER, and, as described most explicitly, Ayahuasca. There are many paths to healing. Your job is to find what is right for you and never give up until you do. Famed writer Dale Carnegie admonished, "Keep your mind open to change all the time. It is only by examining and reexamining your opinions and ideas that you can progress." That open-mindedness will allow information to find you when you are ready to receive it.

Ignite Your Passion

Seeing these new possibilities for your life emerge will help to ignite your passion and move you to action. Maybe you've always wanted to write a book, launch a new business, or find peace of mind. I had previously buried dreams and desires that I didn't possess the confidence to pursue at the time. I remember leaving the retreat and feeling a strong urge to cut off all of my hair. I'd thought of doing this years prior but was too concerned with what people would think or if I could withstand the critical gaze of the nay-sayers. Plus, I hadn't seen my scalp since birth and had no idea if my head was irregularly shaped, so I was afraid that a shaved head would not be a good look for me. But, after doing the self-healing work, I was ready. All of those fears subsided, and I did it. I went to my dad's barber, sat in the chair, and allowed his clippers to glide over my head as I honored that internal nudge. There was a sense that I was no longer hiding, and it felt extraordinary. Do you know I never felt freer in my life? The fear that held me back was actually the door I needed to breakthrough in order to step into a new opportunity.

What doors of opportunity do you need to breakthrough?

My courage grew stronger and stronger. I said goodbye to my hometown and moved across the country to more fully pursue my television and film career as an Actress and Producer. The look that I thought would be met with criticism and close doors actually opened more doors than I could ever imagine, allowing me to star in national commercials and increase my presence in network TV, new media, and feature film. Saying yes to my true desire led to igniting one of my greatest passions and confirmed that listening to my internal voice indeed leads to alignment.

Network with Winners

In order to accomplish great things, we must seek the assistance of those in a position to help us. It's imperative to surround yourself with people who possess a growth mindset, who are doing the work of daily self-improvement, and are about positive, progressive change. There is also immense value in mentorship and coaching from those who have already done what you are seeking to accomplish. Find your tribe and connect with a community of people who are best suited to help you fulfill your life's purpose.

Empower Others

As you take these steps forward, no matter what level of success you've achieved, your experiences have value to those coming behind you. It is each and every one of our responsibility to be a force for good and to help others along the way. Summon the courage to share your story! Open the door for yourself and others. As the great Mahatma Gandhi said, "Be the change you wish to see in the world." Unapologetically say yes to your dreams. Teach by example and open a pathway for others to follow. The radiant energy you emit can be felt throughout the cosmos.

These five simple steps can guide you on your path and help lead to your next breakthrough. I encourage you to come back to this Divine Manifesto on a daily basis. The more you read it, the more you will unveil deeper truths and direction specifically for you. Know that you are not alone in your journey of self-discovery, alignment, and healing. When you allow yourself to SHINE you are able to *Be Proof Of What's Possible.* The world needs you now more than ever!

For access to additional empowering resources for your journey visit **HavilahMalone.com** and Join our mailing list.

Follow our hashtag on social media **#BeProofOfWhatsPossible**

Acknowledgements

My phenomenal mother instilled in me an invaluable lesson her mother taught her - 'Give people their flowers while living.' With deep gratitude, I want to acknowledge every person who supported and encouraged me throughout writing this book. Thank you for providing me a safe space to lay bare my soul and the countless hours of invaluable feedback you provided that brought this work to life. Your very existence and contributions to the betterment of humanity mean more to me than you know!

THANK YOU

- Ezina Leblanc - Musician/Songwriter, Author, and Founder of Billionaire Bandwidth
- Keiyale Osceola - Real Estate Investor and Mompreneur
- Misty Marshall - Actress, Singer/Songwriter, and Director of Empowerment thru Arts, LLC.
- Regina Carver - Transformational Coach and Author, *How Will I Achieve My Goals*
- Salvador Verduzco - Wellness Program Director, Casa De Espíritu
- Sandy Falcon - Social Justice Researcher and Podcast Host, *The Friend I Wish I Had*
- Saundra Richardson - CEO, SERK - *Saundra's Earthy Rich Kitchen*
- Sheila Mac - Host, NBC's *Sheila Mac Show* and Author, *Bootstraps & Bra Straps*
- Stephanie Osborne - Mindfulness Coach and CEO of Meditate New Orleans
- Susan Hemme - Editor-in-Chief, Hemco Publishing
- Susan Lindner - Speaker, CEO, and Founder of Emerging Media
- Toryn Seabrooks - Director and Founder of NovaRay Entertainment

About the Author

Havilah Malone is an inspirational thought leader on a mission to be a catalyst for positive change in over 2 billion people's lives. The multi-talented millennial powerhouse has been featured on FOX, NBC, ABC, CBS and more. The Actress, Motivational Speaker & former Ms. Louisiana Universal currently resides in Los Angeles, CA. Havilah is also the #1 Best Selling Author of, *How to Become a Publicity Magnet: In Any Market via TV, Radio & Print* and co-Author of the Think & Grow Rich children's classic, *The Amazing Adventures of Oliver Hill* based on Napoleon Hill's Success Principles.

Havilah shares her pillars of success with audiences around the world. She has also been featured in numerous films, national TV commercials, HBO's Insecure, and guest starred on NCIS: New Orleans. Ms. Malone is a recipient of the President's Volunteer Service Award Gold Medal, the Women's Prosperity Network "She Rocks Award", and selected as the SBA InnovateHER Challenge Winner. Ms. Malone also holds several professional accreditations including being a Certified Instructor for the Napoleon Hill Foundation and Master Certified Practitioner of NLP (Neuro-Linguistic Programming). Havilah's nurturing spirit, inspirational voice and magnetizing personality inspire people to #BeProofOfWhatsPossible.

For media inquiries or more information on how to book Havilah Malone please visit www.HavilahMalone.com or email ask@HavilahMalone.com

Illustrator: *Zuri Scott* was born in New York and raised in Atlanta, GA. She received her BFA from the Cooper Union's School of Art. While she maintains a practice of illustrating within various genres, she has a passion for many forms of art making, including painting and time-based media production.